AF550349

~~Divorced~~

Beheaded

Ghosted

www.penguin.co.uk

The Ultimate Guide to Dating from the Iconic Wives of Henry VIII

Satu Hämeenaho-Fox

bantam

TRANSWORLD PUBLISHERS
UK | USA | Canada | Ireland | Australia
India | New Zealand | South Africa

Transworld is part of the Penguin Random House group of companies whose addresses can be found at global.penguinrandomhouse.com.
Penguin Random House UK, One Embassy Gardens, 8 Viaduct Gardens, London SW11 7BW
penguin.co.uk

Penguin
Random House
UK

First published in Great Britain in 2026 by Bantam
an imprint of Transworld Publishers

001

Copyright © Satu Hämeenaho-Fox 2026

The moral right of the author has been asserted

This book is a work of fiction and, except in the case of historical fact, any resemblance to actual persons, living or dead, is purely coincidental.

Every effort has been made to obtain the necessary permissions with reference to copyright material, both illustrative and quoted. We apologize for any omissions in this respect and will be pleased to make the appropriate acknowledgements in any future edition.

Penguin Random House values and supports copyright. Copyright fuels creativity, encourages diverse voices, promotes freedom of expression and supports a vibrant culture. Thank you for purchasing an authorized edition of this book and for respecting intellectual property laws by not reproducing, scanning or distributing any part of it by any means without permission. You are supporting authors and enabling Penguin Random House to continue to publish books for everyone. No part of this book may be used or reproduced in any manner for the purpose of training artificial intelligence technologies or systems. In accordance with Article 4(3) of the DSM Directive 2019/790, Penguin Random House expressly reserves this work from the text and data mining exception.

Designed by Bobby Birchall, Bobby&Co.

Printed and bound in Great Britain by Clays Ltd, Elcograf S.p.A.

The authorized representative in the EEA is Penguin Random House Ireland, Morrison Chambers, 32 Nassau Street, Dublin D02 YH68

A CIP catalogue record for this book is available from the British Library

ISBN: 9780857508737

Penguin Random House is committed to a sustainable future for our business, our readers and our planet. This book is made from Forest Stewardship Council® certified paper.

00:05

*'Did I not tell you
that whenever you argue
with the Queen
she is sure to have the
upper hand?'*

ANNE BOLEYN

08:06

Edit

My phone

Henry VIII

King of England

08:07

Contacts Edit

Wives

Catherine of Aragon	2
Anne Boleyn	14
Jane Seymour	26
Anne of Cleves	38
Katherine Howard	50
Katherine Parr	62

Search 

12:45   

Edit

My phone

Catherine of Aragon

Wifey for lifey

12:47

Contacts | Edit

Catherine of Aragon

Phone
1612-1485-71-1536

Address
Peterborough Cathedral, Peterborough

Info
How dare you call me Henry's 'first' wife? I am his only wife. Our marriage was written in the stars as we were only able to find each other after his brother, sadly, dropped dead. If we're being technical, Arthur and I did have a marriage ceremony, but it was never consummated, OK? When Henry became king, he naturally chose me as his queen. Yet after twenty-four years of loyalty, he became thankless. Cruel. Cold-hearted. All because we didn't have a son. A new French fancy caught his eye. When I reminded him of our solemn vows, he threw a huge tantrum, dumped me *and* the Pope, and generally acted like a spoilt child. Well, Henry, I have a temper too. And unlike you, I never, ever change my mind. No matter what your 'Church' of 'England' says, I will go to the grave knowing I am your one true wife.

My boyfriend wants to split up.

We've been together for twenty-four weeks next Tuesday, and now I have no boyfriend and no one to drive me to Comic Con. He didn't even tell me face to face, he sent me a picture of shocked Pikachu captioned 'You when I dump u lmao'. I asked him what he meant because I thought we were together for ever and his only reaction was to thumbs-down the message.
I am devastated.

How do I respond to this?

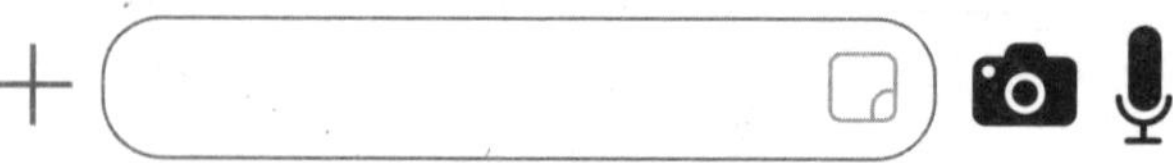

12:55 

Catherine of Aragon

CoA

No. Over your dead body will you let him break up with you. Call for a fresh horse and ride all night to his palace. Have your kinsmen beat down the door. When he agreed to wed, he entered into a pact of blood and honour. You and your Prince (or Princess?) Pikachu (unusual name – French? Prussian?) shall be by each other's side at court until one of you dies. And then you shall be married in heaven.

Anne Boleyn

AB

Sounds like a new babe arrived on the scene . . .

My guy supports Chelsea Football Club and is obsessed with cooking the perfect steak.

I support Forest Green Rovers, the world's first vegan football club, along with my entire, also vegan, family. Should I loosen up and eat a £7 meat-based hot dog with him every Saturday at Chelsea, just to show him I can compromise?

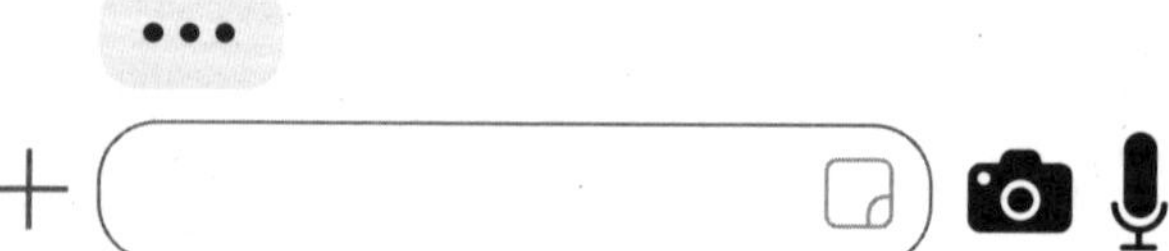

Catherine of Aragon

CoA

Absolutely not.

He should be coming to your football club and eating your choice of food. If you give in like a sad little doormat on this matter, he will think he can walk all over you at home and in great matters of state. Never, ever back down from even the smallest fight in case you set a precedent.

Compromise? I don't know her.

I'm worried that the passion is dying between me and my boyfriend.

We used to go out dancing and spent our annual leave ticking off countries on my bucket list. But now all he does is laze around the house watching jousting videos on his phone. I still want to go out and have fun, but he says he'd rather have a staycation than a city break. We've now hit 400 consecutive nights in. Yes, I have been tracking them. Is this laziness inevitable once he knows you're here to stay?

17:15

Catherine of Aragon

CoA

Ah, the part where you get to know the real person.

When I met Henry, I loved how he was always up for invading France, day or night. After about fifteen years of marriage, he changed. He just seemed to lose interest in international warfare, and in me. I tried everything, including reading to him from the Bible in Latin. Nothing worked. In the end, I just did my own thing and made sure he knew I was here for him when he wanted to get his dancing hose on again. Too bad that didn't work out.

•••

18:22

Hi, queens. I just broke up with the guy I was seeing.

No, don't worry, it was literally only three weeks, and it takes me at least five weeks to fall in love. The problem is that he wants back all the gifts he bought me, and has sent me a Monzo request for a single matcha iced latte he bought me 'as a treat'. I binned those teddies straight away and gave the bespoke couples' snowglobe with our lookalikes in it to the charity shop.

What do I say?

18:32 

Catherine of Aragon

CoA

My Henry has given me many spenny gifts during our long and faithful and only marriage. The idea that he would ask for them back is ludicrous. The only thing that could ever part us is death, and I hope he would bury me in our shared plot with all my pearls, diamonds and 'H+K for ever' merch. Why does your ex-inamorato even want the gifts – he can hardly give them to someone else?

As for the matcha latte, shillings and pence – take it to the Pope.

I think my boyfriend's head has been turned.

I've never been a jealous person, but I can't help but notice he has been liking this one particular girl's pictures a lot. She doesn't look like the loyal and faithful type to me, more of a Ferrari than a Fiat. Not very reliable, in other words. My friends say that he won't go out for a burger when he has steak at home. But that doesn't make any sense to me – I love a burger myself, with triple-cooked chips and a pickle.

Catherine of Aragon

CoA

Your friends are right.

Why would he stray when he has such a good girl at hom–?

Anne Boleyn

AB

I'll take it from here, Cathy.

My darling writer, you call this girl a burger *and* a Ferrari. She sounds like a great time to me. If I were you, I'd start packing my bags straight away. Maybe during this incoming period of singledom you can work on becoming a faster ride with a lot less boot space.

14:45

Edit

My phone

Anne Boleyn

DO NOT ANSWER

14:48

Contacts Edit

Anne Boleyn

Phone
1501-19-05-1536

Address
Tower of London, London

Info
When I was twelve, I was already living at the French court. The English court is so cute and mundane in comparison. When I arrived and met Henry, we knew immediately we were meant for each other. He wanted me body and soul, and I . . . well, I wanted to be queen. Who wouldn't? It started as flirting but quickly got smutty. The one thing I wouldn't do was sleep with him, which obviously drove him wild. I know people hate me for what I did, but I'm not entirely cold-hearted. Henry was a beautiful, powerful man. When we finally got married, we were *that* couple. But he didn't give me a proper chance to provide a son. He even had the audacity to call me a cheat, a liar and a witch. He just wanted what he couldn't have. All that beauty turned to bitterness and that power into poison. He cut off my head and said, 'thank u, next'.

I met a gorgeous, magical, mystical girl in the merch queue at the Chappell Roan concert.

I complained about how hard it was to get tickets and she said it was no big deal for her because her dad runs a record company. My loins were aflame. Obvs, I wanted to marry her, but I somehow played it cool in the moment. Afterwards, I swear I saw her looking at my mini skirt and go-go boots in an appreciative way.

How do I woo her?

06:52 

Anne Boleyn

AB

Firstly, you do not woo.

You have identified a high-value target and they must feel that they have wooed you. You have seen her eyes fall upon certain elements of your attire. Lure her in by posing with these on prominent display at the next recital. She will be consumed by lust, but whatever happens, do not give in to your own womanly sinfulness until you have the tickets firmly in your hands.

11:31

My girlfriend, Annie, recently went on an exchange programme in Paris.

The distance was no problem, we just video-called a lot and she posted all her fun outings on her @annieinparis account. When she came back, she started speaking with a French accent and asked me to call her Angélique. I am happy to go with the name change, but, respectfully, I feel like she's being kind of pretentious and insane. Should I ask her to become Annie again?

11:38 

Anne Boleyn

AB

Becoming French makes everyone more sophisticated. Women often ask me, 'Should I abandon my boyfriend Jack and go to Paris?' and the answer is always yes. Men are such bobolynes. Why would she go back to her old frumpy English demeanour now that she has been improved in every way? You should ask her for style tips and be eternally grateful she did not replace you with a taller man called Jacques.

Be gone from my sight.

•••

11:55

Shall I do a love ritual?

I met a witch who showed me how to say an incantation over a sacred candle to enthral the one I love. I can't quite remember the words, so I think I'll just chant, 'Fancy me, fancy me, fancy me'. The only candle I own has a picture of Dolly Parton as the Virgin Mary. That seems pretty sacred to me, but I'm concerned that I am going to offend the clergy and my witch friends at the same time.

•••

Anne Boleyn

AB

Absolutely conduct your eldritch sorcery if it helps you get what you want.

Your imperfect substitutions may summon the devil, but it seems that you are after a man, so it's the same either way. One caution: you must commit to keeping this witchcraft and your association with hags and enchantresses a secret, but especially from your love object. You'd think they'd be flattered, but you never know how they will take it.

...

Help me with a mystery. I met this lad on an app.

Normally the chats are dry beyond belief, but he asks me questions about my life and shares such sweet, vulnerable thoughts about his family and his career playing e-table tennis. He's so passionate about the sport, I suggested meeting up to play, but he said that playing real-world table tennis would disrupt his training. I said, 'Well, how about a walk round the park?' He said yes but has gone quiet since. I can't stop thinking about him.

13:32

Anne Boleyn

AB

A man after my own heart!

I don't know why everyone doesn't do this. You give people just enough attention so they fall for you, and then pull back. Then they become obsessed with you. I have five or six people chasing me at the moment. I'll get around to picking one of them if it suits me. For example, if they inherit a kingdom or buy a yacht.

Maybe you should become a big investor in e-table tennis?

20:01

I have been learning a lot about attachment styles on TikTok.

I am a classic anxious type who just really wants to be loved and to feel super-close to my queens. I do tend to get kind of disappointed when they can't be, like, everything I need all in one person. I have thrown the *occasional* hissy fit when I feel like they've kept a secret from me. I'm not in the wrong, though? If you love someone, shouldn't you be so close you basically become one and they make sure you are always happy?

20:40 

Anne Boleyn

AB

Henry, I know that's you.

Can you not calm down for a second and let a person live? If I'm sequestered in my own quarters for one single day, it could be for any number of reasons, none of which are banging my lute player or performing black magic. When we were courting, you seemed so cool. I mean, you're literally the king.

Why are you being so insecure and mental? Oh my God, I just can't deal with this right now.

•••

21:58

Edit

My phone

Jane Seymour

My heart

Jane Seymour

Phone
00-1508-2410-1537

Address
St. George's Chapel, Windsor Castle, Berkshire

Info
Everyone always just saw me as a nice girl from a noble family, and without Henry that's all I would ever have been. I was determined to love, honour and obey whoever I was to marry, to be decided by my male relatives. They've got my best interests at heart! I have heard people say Henry wasn't always the nicest man, but he was always lovely to me. He made me feel so safe. For example, I was feeling anxious after he beheaded Anne Boleyn, so he made sure we got married quickly so I would feel secure again. Occasionally, I wonder whether our love would have lasted without our little boy and heir, Edward, but I guess that's something I'll never know. I believe Henry loved me very much and, by making me his queen, made it so people will hopefully remember little old me long after I'm gone. I can only pray that one day he will be buried right by my side so we can rest together for eternity.

22:29

I know it's politically incorrect, but I yearn for the tradwife life.

I have seen all the videos of women wandering through meadows wearing white dresses and not having to create Trello boards for the shareholder meeting. I feel like I am destined to harvest my own salad rather than paying £10 for it. As far as I understand, meadows are full of free salad, and women without their own money are treated super-nicely and kindly by their husbands. Shall I quit my job to pursue this life?

Jane Seymour

JS

Well, yes!

I always knew I would be a wife and mother. When I think about it, I've never actually met a woman who wasn't those things. As a wife and queen, I know that my only role in life is pleasing the king and incubating an heir. Like you, I sometimes pretend to make food, as a joke. It's a little life, but I love it!

When I give the king a little boy, I truly feel like my life will be complete and I can die of happiness.

My boyfriend of two months has a lot more dating experience than me.

He has two 'big exes' while this is my first proper relationship. His exes sound like total nightmares, to be honest. He says the first one was 'crazy' and obsessed with him, and the second one was just a psycho witch. I'm glad he's finally found me, but I worry that I won't be enough for such an emotionally mature man.

•••

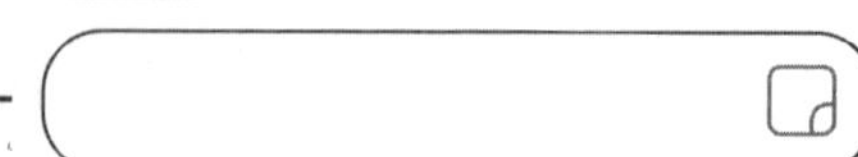

Jane Seymour

JS

Just be yourself! It's clear that he was very unlucky with those first two women. Maybe they put a spell on him? It's not his fault that they were such awful wives. Hardly queens at all when you think about it. If they had made sure to meet every single one of his needs, day and night, he wouldn't speak about them that way. Take heart!

He probably never thinks about them any more, now that he's with you.

14:44

I really want to make my boyfriend's birthday special this year.

He's been kind of down after falling off his jousting charger and hurting himself. I did say maybe he should leave the extreme sports to the under-thirties and he got really offended. I felt bad for criticizing his hobby and I want to make it up to him.

•••

14:50

Jane Seymour

JS

The best way to show you are truly sorry would be to make a custom cake in the style of a noble knight. I prefer to gather ears of wheat at dawn, then grind them into the finest flour. After stopping in at the henhouse for eggs and milking a cow, I would ask the palace pastry cook to make it and then present it to my most beloved husband and king.

Make sure to sprinkle flour on to your dress to make it more believable.

•••

I have watched every series of *MAFS: Australia* and every episode of *Love is Blind*, even the Swedish version.

When they say, 'I just feel really ready for marriage', I feel the same. I just met someone the old-fashioned way, volunteering at a sea-turtle sanctuary, and we had a whirlwind romance. He got down on the sand, in between the turtle-egg shell casings, and asked me to marry him. My friends say it's 'too quick' and 'Not this again; remember Raoul', but I am trying to ignore the haters.

Jane Seymour

JS

I got engaged quickly myself.

The circumstances of falling in love are not always ideal and people need to get over it! Sometimes they live in South London and it takes one hour and forty-five minutes by bus to get to their house. My own love story is a rose with a thorn. Henry had actually beheaded his former wife the day before, and they hadn't yet washed her blood from the stones. I encouraged everyone in our circle to move on from the past and stop bringing negative energy.

When we married two weeks later, everyone was so happy for us.

I have a short pixie cut that I absolutely love.

The only problems are the cost of regular trips to the hairdresser and my boyfriend's preferences. He can't stop going on about hair. I assume he wants that long, flowing hair look. I resent his ideas about the beauty standard but otherwise he's a good partner.

Should I grow it out?

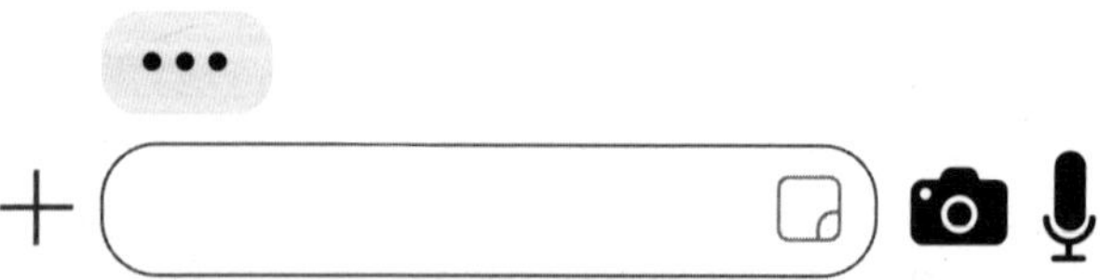

15:57 

Jane Seymour

JS

Why not look good for your partner?!

Anne Boleyn

AB

Oh, shut up, Jane. I have spent many hours in front of the glass plucking my hairline and pinching my cheeks to improve my appearance. I only went through these ridiculous rituals to get what I wanted: advancement. If it benefits you, go for it.

Anne of Cleves

AoC

Hello, dear sister queens 😇. You're both wrong of course. You will never meet the standards of the men. It is advised not to try.

21:58   

Edit

My phone

Anne of Cleves

Anne 2 new

22:01

Contacts Edit

Anne of Cleves

Phone

229-1515-167-1557

Address

Westminster Abbey, Westminster, London

Info

Two years after Jane died, Henry was a single Pringle ready to mingle. There's not much to do in Cleves, so when Henry and I were set up together I was so excited! Henry asked for portraits and even sent one of his closest advisors, Thomas Cromwell, to take a look at me. Obviously, everyone reassured him I was stunning. Typical man: when he met me he threw a tantrum because it turned out I was 'not his type'. He was so grossed-out by my face, he annulled the marriage. I thank my lucky stars that my royal nepo status saved my head, literally! Henry had wanted to create an alliance with my Protestant family, and, even though we didn't stay married, he couldn't risk angering them. Once I got over the rejection and he decided not to behead me, we actually became good friends and I got a bunch of land to make up for it. Still, being called a catfish sucks a little. At least I ended up with the riches.

I am thinking of asking the girl I'm seeing to be exclusive.

I have never had a girlfriend before, and ever since I first laid eyes on her at the ceramics fair my heart has been entirely hers. But what if she is dating many other people, possibly many other ceramicists? She's so beautiful and her hand-throwing is so consistent. I don't want to find out that she doesn't love me back.

08:35 

Anne of Cleves

This beautiful pottery maiden seems to like you back, even though you haven't described the standard of your own ceramics. Are you as strong as earthenware, or is your ego as fragile as porcelain? It sounds like you are trying to avoid taking a risk for the woman you love. Perhaps she'll want you and only you. Or perhaps she wants to share her love with many people.

Either way, you'll have to accept her truth and make space in your spare room for all her bowls.

My style is light academia with a twist of cyberpunk, which suits me as I'm a video-game developer.

When I got together with my boyfriend, I thought he liked how I looked, but now he's dropping hints about me dressing 'more feminine', like his mates' girlfriends. I don't know what this means. Like, shall I put on a flower crown? Dress like a Disney princess? Wear only pink?

•••

14:59

Anne of Cleves

Trust me, alienating the male gaze leads to riches. Some styling suggestions: a shapeless knitted hat and orthopaedic shoes such as a travelling privy cleaner might don. Then, ideally, this knave will spurn your bed, leaving more hours for your development of games. However, be aware, many an empty word has been said about how a lady should appear in the streets, when the gentleman takes full enjoyment of her abundance between the sheets.

19:09

My new boyfriend is allergic to cats and says he can't keep dating someone with a feline friend.

I think my cat, Professor Fluffy, has picked up on the tension. He shoots daggers at Alfie with his huge, luminous eyes and strategically threw up on his Xbox controller. I told my best friend about the problem and she said, 'So when are you getting rid of him?' I would never get rid of Professor Fluffy. How can I bring about peace?

19:14

Anne of Cleves

AoC

It sounds like you are caught between two bratty boyfriends here. Has Alfie heard of allergy medication? And has Professor Fluffy heard of boundaries? The problem here is that you are pre-contracted to the Professor, so you do owe him something. When you make a commitment, you have to stick to it. Professor Fluffy needs you in a way that Alfie never could.

But I don't love the Professor's territorial behaviour and I think he should quit it.

22:24

I'm deciding on a really nice main picture for my dating-app profile.

Do you think it should be of me at a party, out in nature, or doing my favourite activity of creating engaging content for my followers? I'm very conventionally pretty, so I want to try to limit who chooses me. I actually heard the app can crash if someone gets over 10,000 swipes, and I'd feel awful if I stopped people from finding love.

+

22:34 

Anne of Cleves

I mean, what is prettiness when you really think about it? After all, love looks not with the eyes but with the mind. Perhaps if the radiance of your beauty is so overpowering, you should just post a birthday cake, or a leaf, or a unit of engaging content that does not show your extremely pretty face.

What about a poll asking if people would rather get the plague or kiss a follower of the Pope? That would really get me thinking!

Dear queens, I met my girlfriend in r/animalssmiling.

We both just love to see our animal-kingdom bros beaming up at us. She lives in Westphalia, but after a few months of chatting we were so in love she decided to come over for a two-week visit. Well, she is here now. And it turns out an appreciation for cute mammals is not enough for a relationship. She's in the other room browsing our subreddit, which I now want to leave. How do I get rid of her?

Anne of Cleves

I used to think that a shared interest or goal, such as smiling animals or uniting all of Europe under the one true faith, was enough for a marriage. When I met Henry, we even had a tentative make-out session, which I thought might blossom into love. After all, why would you kiss someone you're not interested in? He never gave us a real chance. Can you at least take this girl out to see the sights before you spurn her? Please don't send her straight home to her father.

Katherine Howard

Auntie Anne, you are so funny. Letter writer, I know exactly what you mean. Only simps worry about shared interests, I just want to know if they're into me.

09:12

Edit

My phone

Katherine Howard

Katherine 2 Tinder

09:45

Contacts

Edit

Katherine Howard

Phone

21-23-13-021542

Address

Tower of London, London

Info

Hiiii! So, after my parents died (I know, boohoo, but it was ages ago), I had to go and stay with a random auntie. There were loads of other girls there, and no one really paid any attention to us, so we got to do what we liked, which was great. There were even fit boys around, if you count servants and dancing masters. Some of the other girls were quite jelly of me because I was the most popular. But that was nothing compared to when the actual King of England asked me out. *SCREAM*. So I said yes and went to live at court, with his missus down the corridor. After she got binned off, I thought it would be really fun, but it wasn't. Most of the court people are old and serious, and Henry just wanted to cuddle and get his gross illnesses taken care of. I was like, I'm seventeen, bro! So basically I did start hooking up with a few other lads from around the court and unfortunately Henry found out. I said I was sorry, but he didn't want to talk about it, just literally had me beheaded.

06:14

My love language is physical touch and words of affirmation.

I've been trying to persuade my queen, I mean my wife, to give me more back massages and to tell me I look good in my new velvet jerkin. She only gives very half-hearted backrubs. I also suspect she finds the large open wound on my leg that never heals disgusting and not 'just part of the man I love', as she claims.

06:22 

Katherine Howard

This is so strange, your wife could literally be me! My family made me marry this old, gross man who also has a huge suppurating wound that never heals. I find it absolutely rank. I sometimes force myself to tend to his decrepit body and make sure to hide how I really feel about him at all times, so that my family can keep getting riches from him.

But that's just me . . . I'm sure your wife loves you just the way you are.

08:37

My latest hyperfixation is making miniature dollhouse rooms.

I just cannot get enough of making teensy coffee shops with teensy tables, teensy chairs and teensy digital nomads. My latest creation was a diorama of the Timothée Chalamet lookalike competition where Timothée Chalamet actually turned up. It was a masterpiece until my partner accidentally-on-purpose trod on it. I'm furious. They say it was an accident and they are not jealous of Timothée Chalamet. Should I trash one of their prized possessions in retaliation?

Katherine Howard

Oh my gosh, I would be so annoyed?

I don't think you should destroy anyone's things, even if you're really angry. I never had a lot of my own things and I don't like it when people mess with my stuff. Maybe you need a new partner who won't feel threatened by throngs of Timothées, especially little miniature ones.

By the way, who is your friend Timothée? He sounds nice. Do you have his portrait?

16:01

I got a date with an actual 10/10.

You would fall down dead at how sharp his jawline is. He is the CEO (!) of a company that turns plastic bottles into new plastic bottles with inspirational feminist quotes on them. His dad, the Duke of England, gave him the money to get started – such a kind family! So, the only small problem is that on our date he never asked me any questions about myself. Maybe he's hot and interesting enough for both of us?

16:13

Katherine Howard

OMG, he sounds amazing. Your friends will be mega-jealous you bagged him.

If I were you, I would make sure everyone sees you together, so they know you have snagged a hottie. Then I would be on the hunt for another companion who asks you questions about yourself and has no money and isn't hot, so you'll have everything you need!

19:12

Hiiii!

I (17f) have been with my boyfriend (49m) for–

Katherine Parr

KP NO.

Catherine of Aragon

In the ideal relationship, the woman is slightly older and more mature, so she can explain to her partner where he is going wrong.

Anne Boleyn

AB Not even I think this is worth it, even if he's a billionaire.

19:34

Jane Seymour

JS

When you're dating with intention, you have to pick a person who you can achieve all your life goals with, together, until one of you dies. The life–death ratio here seems a little squiffy to me, if that makes sense!

Anne of Cleves

AoC

Go back to school, sweetie.

Katherine Howard

KH

Some older guys are hot. Is he hot? He's probably not hot, is he?

Anne Boleyn

KP

Sigh.

Dear queens, I feel like no one ever likes me.

I'm one of those people who is ordinary. I work a normal, boring job and like relaxing at home after work with a cup of tea and a book. OK, with a cup of tea and my phone. What if I never find someone who loves me the way I am?

Catherine of Aragon

What does liking have to do with it?

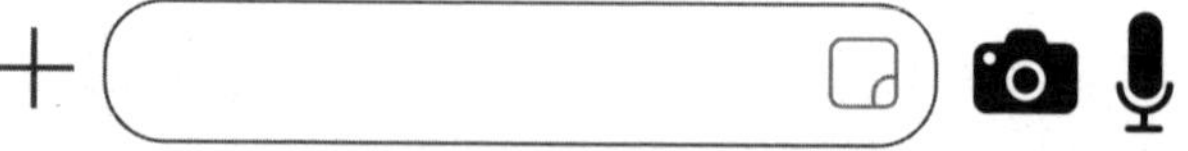

01:03 

Anne Boleyn

AB Sounds like a you problem.

Jane Seymour

JS I'm so sorry, being unlovable sounds so hard. Good luck, babe!

Anne of Cleves

AoC Wonderful!

Katherine Howard

KH On a date but will reply later xx

Katherine Parr

KP Sweetheart, you are beautiful inside and out. It's just a matter of time. For now, concentrate on loving yourself and love will find you.

Edit

My phone

Katherine Parr

Work wife

16:40

Contacts

Edit

Katherine Parr

Phone
081502-591548

Address
Sudeley Castle Chapel, Winchcombe, Gloucestershire

Info
By the time I met Henry, he was in struggle mode. His old jousting injury was hurting all the time and that poor teen bride he married hadn't solved his mid-life crisis. I'm not deluded. Our marriage was a sensible one, not a passionate one. I'd been married before, so I knew what most men want: a mother figure to tend to their needs. Henry's needs included ruling England when he was away at war and not undermining the Church of England. I did the best I could. When Henry died, I finally felt free. I'd done more duty as a wife than anyone could have asked. This time it was my choice, and I chose Thomas Seymour. He was as much a typical man as they all are, but he was *my* typical man. We had a few stolen months of happiness before I died giving birth to our child. RIP me, Henry's last queen.

18:22 

I've been asked to pose as the loving girlfriend of a popular celebrity to quell rumours that he is gay.

It sounds like an obvious no, but hear me out. I have loved his music for years and even had a poster of him on my wall as a teenager. In an ideal world he could come out, but in the meantime I can hang out with my actual idol and get paid for everyone to think we're shagging. Actually, I would do it all for free.

Should I go for it?

Katherine Parr

All marriages are a burden in one way or another. The circumstances of this union are indeed unusual, but I admire your desire to help a bard you esteem so highly. Music is such a balm after a long day of pretending to agree with everything your husband says about the Church of England. To spend your days with one who shares your interests and will make no demands in the marital bed sounds like a kind of heaven.

One can only wish that your minstrel could show himself at court in his true colours.

Have you noticed that the apps are kind of a ghost town these days?

I feel like when I started on them, I was at least getting dates. But now everyone just wants to chat endlessly and going on a real date seems to scare people to death! Is it my looks, my personality, or are all men on the surface of the earth to blame?

20:55 

Katherine Parr

After a few rounds of heartbreak and disappointment, it can feel like love is impossible. I know this only too well after four husbands. I never had any control over what they did, only my own actions. The gap between what I hoped each husband would be and who they were was vast. How can a man ever understand a woman, let alone a king understand a queen?

But I filled the space between us with love.

Queens, I am a catch. I own my own home, I'm a doctor, and I'm looking to settle down.

I asked my female co-workers to confirm that I am handsome. The weird thing is, I can't seem to find the right lovely lady. I'm drawn to classy, high-achieving women with long glossy hair like a human My Little Pony. Maybe a doctor but in a less prestigious area of medicine than mine.

Why can't I seem to lock one down?

+

Katherine Parr

Your dream woman sounds wonderful. Indeed, one in a million! Such a woman would have their choice of many suitors, I am sure. It's possible – just possible – that this small cohort of potential wives is in fact choosing those other men who like fun, confident and socially influential partners.

There is no accounting for taste. Just throw your hat in the ring and hope it lands on a lady with horse-like features.

I'm a fully grown Capricorn with my own flat and a socially-anxious cockapoo called Geoff.

I am not one to swoon. But when I was fifteen, I had a fling with a boy at summer camp. When I went home, I wrote him loads of emails, but Caleb never responded. GUESS WHO just joined my company? It's him. I jokingly asked him over corporate drinks why he never responded to my emails, and he swept his golden hair back and said, 'I don't know how to use a computer.' We work in tech, but never mind. He's even more gorgeous than I remember. I have to go for it, right?

Katherine Parr

You sound like you've worked really hard to be the practical, sensible one. You've done really well. But maybe in your heart of hearts you always hoped you'd find Caleb again. He sounds like he could really use someone like you. And he sounds like he enjoys a simple life. This might help Geoff with his anxiety?

There is nothing like a first love. I say go for it. Life is so short.

I've been reflecting lately on all the queens I have loved and lost in my life.

When I was a young man, I thought I'd live for ever. I fell in love hard and fast, but I also fell out of love just as easily and never looked back. I thought I was the prize catch and they were lucky to be with me. I confused kindness with weakness. Now that I have two daughters, I regret how I treated women. How can I ever make amends and get everyone to say I am a good guy?

14:33 

Katherine Parr

KP

Hello, Henry my love.

This is a lot of personal growth for you and I'm very proud. But I'm afraid this is a common story for men like you. By the time they realize that women are people, their ladykilling days are over and their thoughts on women and dating have become completely irrelevant. The only thing you can do is treat your current queen as well as you possibly can and try to be a good guy for the rest of your life . . . however long that might be.

...

Satu Hämeenaho-Fox has written books about many people whose artistry and/or clothes she likes, including Taylor Swift, Harry Styles, Zendaya and Jane Austen. She has also written children's books on art and fashion history for New York's Metropolitan Museum of Art. She is the co-founder of the *Swiftian Theory* newsletter.